**Life of Contentment**

# Orangebooks Publication

Smriti Nagar, Bhilai, Chhattisgarh - 490020

Website: **www.orangebooks.in**

---

**© Copyright, 2022, Author**

All rights reserved. No part of this book may be reproduced, stored in a retrieval system, or transmitted, in any form by any means, electronic, mechanical, magnetic, optical, chemical, manual, photocopying, recording or otherwise, without the prior written consent of its writer.

**First Edition, 2022**

# LIFE *of* CONTENTMENT

How To Have A More Satisfying Life
And Not Be Tied To Expectations

# Mustafa Mun

**OrangeBooks Publication**
www.orangebooks.in

# LIVE A LIFE OF
# CONTENTMENT

## How To Have a More Satisfying Life and Not Be Tied To Expectations

# Disclaimer

This eBook has been written for informational purposes only. Every effort has been made to make this eBook as complete and accurate as possible. However, there may be mistakes in typography or content. Also, this eBook provides information only up to the publishing date. Therefore, this eBook should be used as a guide - not as the ultimate source.

The purpose of this eBook is to educate. The author and publisher make no warranty that the information in this eBook is complete and are not liable for any errors or omissions.The author and publisher will have no liability or responsibility to any person or entity for any loss or damage caused or alleged to be caused by this ebook, whether directly or indirectly.

This eBook offers information and is designed for educational purposes only. You should not rely on this information as a substitute for, nor does it replace professional medical advice, diagnosis, or treatment.

# Table of Contents

Introduction .................................................................. 2

### Chapter – 1
**Understand Satisfaction Is A Mindset** ....................... 5
- What Does It Mean To Be Satisfied? ......................... 6
- Lack, Abundance, and Satisfaction ............................ 7
- Practice Satisfaction .................................................. 8

### Chapter - 2
**Learn The Difference Between Expectations And Wants** ...................................................................... 11
- Turning Wants Into Expectations Can Lead To Satisfaction Troubles .............................................. 12
- Losing Satisfaction From Lost Experiences ............. 13

### Chapter - 3
**Self-love Isn't Easy** ..................................................... 17
- Self-love Doesn't Have To Mean Stagnation, Just Satisfaction ...................................................... 19
- Making Self-love Easier ........................................... 20
    - Take Yourself Out For Some Self-care ............... 20
    - Be Around People Who Love You ...................... 21

### Chapter - 4
**Tame Your Inner Voice** ............................................. 23
- Step 1: Focus On What The Inner Voice Is Telling You .............................................................. 24

- Step 2: Counter Each Negative Phrase With Something Positive .................................................. 24
- Having An Out Of Control Positive Inner Voice ..... 26

# Chapter - 5
## Less Is More .............................................................. 28
- How Less Is More Can Lead To Satisfaction ........... 29
  - This Applies To Everything ................................. 30

# Chapter - 6
## Know When Social Media Is Toxic ........................... 33
- What Is Toxic Social Media? .................................... 34
- How To Overcome Toxic Social Media ................... 35
- Clearing Out The Errant Toxicity ............................. 35

# Chapter - 7
## Don't Be Afraid To Try New Things ........................ 38
- The Base Level Of Happiness ................................... 39
- What New Things Should I Try? .............................. 40

# Chapter - 8
## Life Is A Journey, Not A Destination ....................... 43
- Focus On What Really Matters ................................. 44
- Don't Be Afraid To Rest And Just Be Content ........ 44
- Have Some Fun ......................................................... 45
- **Conclusion** .................................................................. 48

# Introduction

# Introduction

We all want to be satisfied, even though we know some people who will never be that way, and others who see satisfaction as a foreign emotion that they can't hope to ever feel. However, whenever it comes to being content and living a life free from want and worry, it's actually much easier to do so that you think. Even though our wants and desires are physical, the life of contentment we seek starts in our minds.

By using strategies such as taming our inner critic who always seems to push us towards lack, to learning to love yourself by controlling what goes in your heads and hearts, there are a wide variety of mental strategies that can help you become more content, and be satisfied with where you are.

Now, this does bear repeating as it is one of the main themes of the book: Satisfaction does not equal stagnation, and it is perfectly healthy to be content, and still have the desire and the means for growth. But you can never build abundance out of lack and discomfort, so in order to properly grow, we need to reach the middle ground of being satisfied with where we are.

Along the way, this book contains exercises and examples to help get you into a life of contentment, so you can start living that style of life right away without any issues. If you keep an open mind and understand what this book is trying to tell you, then you will be 100% ready to become more content, regardless of what your situation might be.

Understand
Satisfaction
Is A Mindset

# Understand Satisfaction Is A Mindset

Have you ever met someone with an insane desire to succeed with something? They might strive to get perfect grades in every single class, might want to get a perfect body, or go on dozens upon dozens of dates just to find 'the one.' These people seem to have it all, and yet for every victory they gain, they want to climb another mountain. For every step forward their feet take, their minds are already three steps ahead in the future.

You also might have met people who aren't growing, but still have a desire. They want the dream body, amazing grades, the perfect romance, and if the world would just give it to them, they could make the most of it! These are the people who want to be satisfied and want their lives to improve, as long as someone else does the work for them and simply hands them the result. They live ten steps in the future while their feet haven't moved an inch.

Still, you have probably met people with no desire to succeed more than they already have. They have their life and while it might not be perfect or everything the world tells us we should want, it's good enough. They might strive for small goals or want to make tiny improvements, but they really don't care either way. If things go well, then things go well, and if things dip a bit, then they are just thankful the pendulum didn't swing too far in the wrong direction.

All three of these types of people have one thing in common that drives how they behave in life. It isn't wealth, education, opportunity, their home life, or the hand that life ended up dealing to them. It actually isn't anything physical at all, it's their level of satisfaction, how they use it, and their mindset around it.

## What Does It Mean To Be Satisfied?

The dictionary defines satisfaction as "the fulfillment of one's wishes, expectations, or needs, or the pleasure derived from this." All of us are satisfied every single day, especially when it comes to basic needs. When we are hungry, thirsty, or tired, we eat, drink, and sleep until we don't need anymore. Too little of these needs and we feel bad and act badly towards others, while too much of these needs can throw our bodies off.

However, whenever we get just enough to where we don't need anymore, we can be satisfied and go about our day. Satisfaction is something that keeps us content, where we are fine with where we are and we don't need to have any more. But the level of satisfaction isn't the same for everyone, and in fact, it is a mindset that is different for each person.

What satisfies one person might not be enough or might be too much for another. That's why people with a growth mindset, for example, are almost never content to rest on their laurels and want to seek out the newest challenges. However, for people without a growth mindset, they would be satisfied with any one of the things a high achiever could do and likely wouldn't feel the need to do anymore.

Since satisfaction is a mindset, that means you can choose to be satisfied right here and now. You don't need anything special, but of course, that is easier said than done. Still, the fact that you have the ability to choose to be satisfied and content with anything should be empowering to you. The situation that you are in doesn't get to determine your level of happiness anymore, but instead that job falls to your mind and your mindset .

## Lack, Abundance, and Satisfaction

It can be difficult to be satisfied when you want something or when lack is staring you down. For example , let's use everyone's favorite topic: money. Whenever bills and debts and rising prices are constantly hitting you in the face, you might wonder how you could ever be satisfied with that!

However, one way to be satisfied is to look at what you have.

Chances are, no matter how tight things end up getting, you will always find a way to put food on the table and keep your roof over your head. So, focus on that, be grateful that while times are hard you don't have a lack of food or shelter. Be grateful that you have your health and education about money. Be grateful that you have the dedication to save and the wisdom to know how to make every dollar go the furthest and do the most that it can.

Gratitude is one of the keys to developing a satisfied mindset, and it doesn't just work for lack. It can also work for abundance too. If you find yourself having an abundance of good fortune, take a moment to be satisfied with what you have or be satisfied with what the abundance will bring you.

Having extra money, for example, might mean that your debts are paid off, that you can take a vacation, or that you can improve your living standards. You might be able to get something or take advantage of an opportunity that was otherwise out of your reach. This can be a great time to pause and be satisfied with where you are. Congratulations! You have more than enough. You can take advantage of that. You don't have to worry.

Keep satisfaction and gratitude with you in times of abundance and lack, and you'll notice that things won't seem as stressful as they once were.

## Practice Satisfaction

Finally, like any other mindset, you will need to practice it. Take the time each day to be satisfied, even if it is with regards to small things. Just focus on what you can be content with, what you are grateful for, and what you have enough of. If you can do it for small things, then you might be able to do it for bigger things as well.

While practicing a mindset might seem a little silly, you can call up feelings of satisfaction and gratitude on command, which can be pretty powerful whenever you are facing lack and scarcity. Being able to center yourself with satisfaction is often enough to keep you from falling down a rabbit hole of feeling terrible when life starts to mess with you.

After all, haven't we been down that rabbit hole enough? And the whole reason you are reading this book is to ensure you live a satisfied life, and that means minimizing despair and seeing the positive in all aspects of life.

# Learn The Difference Between Expectation And Wants

# Learn The Difference Between Expectations And Wants

Wants and expectations might seem pretty similar on the surface, but there is a difference between them... just like with satisfaction, it all comes back to your mindset. For example, let's say you go to a new restaurant. You know nothing about it except for the smells coming from the kitchen and the name on the door, but you want a hamburger.

On the other hand, what if you walked into the same burger place you've been to a thousand times and had the intention of ordering your favorite hamburger, made just the way you like it?

In the first scenario, you didn't know if the restaurant served burgers, you didn't know if the place even had the type of hamburger you liked! You just knew you wanted a burger, but outside circumstances were going to determine if you got the burger. The second scenario had one thing different, you knew the hamburger was there, you just had to order it.

There was no want, no doubt, no worry... You just had to walk to the counter and place the same order, and barring some act of God, you were going to get the burger. You expected it, and we can't want what we expected.

Expectations are as easy as breathing, we all know that as humans, if we breathe in and out, we stay alive. We don't even need to think about breathing because it is something that our bodies do naturally. We don't 'want' to breathe or worry that one day the oxygen isn't going to fulfill our needs. Instead, we know we will get what we need if we perform the action.

Expectations are all well and good, but how does this tie into satisfaction?

## Turning Wants Into Expectations Can Lead To Satisfaction Troubles

Whenever you were younger, did you ever hear adults tell you that something was a 'privilege and not a right?' Most of the time, it might have had to do with electronics or some other reward, where you could have the reward as long as you followed certain rules, otherwise it would be taken away.

Well, as adults, we seem to have had the same lesson taught to us, only this time it has to deal with wants and expectations.

Whenever we turn wants into expectations, particularly unrealistic expectations, we can lose out on being satisfied. For example, let's take a promotion at your job as an example.

Whatever your job might be, you might not be satisfied with it. You might want to make more money, get a promotion, do more important work and less busy work, or really show your boss that you are the best employee this company has ever had.

These are things you want. You want more money, to be promoted, to do better work, to do well in the eyes of your boss, and these wants are good.

They can motivate you to go above and beyond, communicate more, step into the shoes of a leader, and allow you to think more deeply about the work you do. The problem is, whenever these wants turn into expectations. There's a difference between wanting more money and expecting it, or wanting to have your name called for a promotion and expecting that promotion.

Because whenever we don't get what we want, we might be bummed and might use the disappointment to try better. When we don't get what we expected, the emotions often turn to anger and resentment, as if everything we should have gotten has been snatched away. So, instead of trying harder to better ourselves, we become enraged at the people or situations who have taken away what we deserve and what is rightfully ours .

## Losing Satisfaction From Lost Experiences

Having our expectations denied can make us focus on the lack that we are experiencing, which ties us to the expectations. If you lose out on a promotion that you were expecting for instance, you might find that you are angry, you start being resentful towards your job and boss, and you might start doing things that will keep the promotion out of your grasp.

Because we are constantly focusing on the lack that we have, we will undoubtedly feel less satisfied. So how do you avoid this? How do you avoid making everything an expectation and getting tied to the outcome? Well, there are two things you can do. The first is to let go of the outcome, and the second is to search for proof .

Letting out and having outcome independence is something most self-development books will talk about in greater detail, but the main point is to focus on the journey and what you can control, and not on what you can't. For example, in the case of a promotion, you can't control who your boss will pick or what they will look for, but you can focus on being a good employee and showcasing promotable qualities.

If you are promoted, great, but if you aren't, then you are at least being a good employee, which will have its own benefits for you down the line. With this, your satisfaction doesn't hinge on something you can't control, but rather the satisfaction of what you can control- such as a job well done.

Or you can look for proof that validates your expectations. Going back to the hamburger example, you went to the restaurant that sells hamburgers and ordered the same burger that you have had several times over. You know the restaurant in question stocks your favorite, and you don't need to worry about it. You have proof.

Look for the same evidence with your desires. If you know that a certain action or series of actions has gotten other people promotions or extra raises or benefits, then try to take those same actions and replicate the results. They might not always work out, but if they do, then you have the proof needed to make a wish an expectation.

# Self-love Isn't Easy

The concept of loving yourself is supposed to be very easy, and just like with the practice of gratitude, it is one of the things that will help you create a more satisfied life. However, loving yourself isn't easy, and there are several internal and external reasons for that. Thankfully, there are also several ways to overcome that reasoning and start the practice of loving yourself just like you love any other person or animal in your life.

Self-Love is seeing value in yourself, caring for yourself with good self-care habits, and treating yourself with respect. It should be easy, it really should be, especially since you can mirror how you treat other people with self-love as well.

However, even some of the nicest people on the planet suffer from a lack of self-love, which should tell you it is harder than you might think.

For starters, self-love is constantly being attacked by the world around us. While a chapter about the dangers of too much and the wrong types of social media is present later in this book, it's worth a mention here. How are you supposed to love yourself when everyone else is relentlessly chasing down an image of perfection?

Take your body, for example. There's nothing wrong with wanting to improve the way you look; wanting to be healthier, lose weight, or maybe get some more muscles. However, so many people come at it from a place of hatred for their bodies. They look at all their imperfections and state: "I'm so fat/ugly/unwanted/hideous" or "I'd only be good looking if I could just get rid of my fat stomach, or the weight around my thighs, or the extra ten pounds."

This isn't helped by seeing social media photos all over the internet, or even by seeing people walking around who are healthier than you or who have the body you desire. Often, instead of letting that motivate us, we instead compare ourselves to other people and bemoan that we can never be like them.

We don't think that those photos are airbrushed, edited, primped and preened, or that some of those healthy people have done very unhealthy things to radically change their bodies, we just focus on the difference.

In focusing on that difference, we forget to show compassion for where we are or focus on how we can change our bodies. We forget to love ourselves and, in forgetting that love, we forget how to want to improve ourselves.

## Self-Love Doesn't Have To Mean Stagnation, Just Satisfaction

A lot of people seem to think that if we love where we are, then that means that we are doomed to stagnate. Instead, we have to hate where we are and have a desire to grow, and that's the only way we can change. However, while the hate- and anger-based approach may work in the short term or for certain types of people, it rarely works in the long run.

Instead, we need to treat ourselves like children. How many times have parents said "We love you and we want what is best for you?" How many parents love their children regardless of whether they get 1st place or 50th? They are satisfied with whatever their children put out, as long as they do their best and keep on moving forward, and we need to treat ourselves the same way.

Self-love doesn't condemn us to where we are, but instead gives us a foundation to build upon. Going back to getting healthier, which sounds better for long-term growth and health: Hating your body and vowing to get fit like all the people on the internet tell you to do, or loving where you are and accepting that you can become better and want to improve?

Having a base and a bedrock of satisfaction can get you moving far more than having a base of anger and hatred for yourself, but how do you start loving yourself?

## Making Self-love Easier

How would you treat someone you would like to woo or fall in love with? How do you treat someone you are in love with?

What do you do if someone you love is having a rough time of it? Looking at how you treat others can prove a perfect guideline to how to treat yourself.

One of the first steps to self-love is watching what you tell yourself and what you think throughout the day. Do you constantly put yourself down, bemoan that you can't do anything right, or shower yourself with angry put-downs and insults? That's not how you would treat a loved one, and it is certainly not how you should treat yourself.

It sounds silly, but if you choose to watch what you say for a week and make an effort to change the dialogue of your inner voice, you will see some real changes in your satisfaction levels. More of the inner voice will be covered in the next chapter.

### Take Yourself Out For Some Self-Care

Often, whenever we aren't satisfied and we don't love ourselves, we find ourselves stressed out and overwhelmed. When this happens, we need to focus on self-care in order to recharge our batteries and focus on recovering and forgetting about all that is bugging us. So maybe take yourself out on a date! Go somewhere you've always wanted to go, do something that brings you joy, and just treat yourself kindly for a change.

Chances are, you will be very satisfied with the self-care you have just given yourself, and you will also find that your stress levels have gone down as well. It's often night and day what these date nights can do for your physical health, mental health, and levels of satisfaction, so don't skimp on them. You might find that you have a higher capacity for self-love than you previously thought!

**Be Around People Who Love You**

One of the best ways to boost your self-love and self-esteem is to be around people who love you. Spending time with friends, family, a significant other, or all three can really boost your feelings of worthiness and self-love. These people care about you, like what you like, and want to do things that make you happy. If you need a quick mental health boost, then take the time to call some friends or loved ones and watch your mood take off. Plus, they might even be able to help you out with your self-care, because they do know what you like and might have some ideas.

# Tame Your Inner Voice

# Tame Your Inner Voice

Whenever it comes to living a life of contentment, your inner voice can be your biggest ally or your harshest critic, either pushing you forward to find what makes you content, or holding you back and preventing you from truly being happy. For either of these outcomes, too much of an untamed internal voice can be dangerous, so learning how to tame that inner voice is often very helpful in your journey towards contentment.

Your inner voice might seem impossible to tame because it never seems to shut up. Every time you try to strive for something, it is their speaking, telling you that you can't do it or that you need to focus on something easier, something you actually can do. If you are seeking to change your mindset from one of scarcity to one of abundance, then you can definitely expect your inner voice to snap at you.

So, how do you tame your inner voice and ensure that it works with you and not against you? There are a few steps you can take, and while they might seem like they take a lot of time and effort, you might find that it is all worth it once your inner voice starts telling you what you want to hear.

## Step 1: Focus On What The Inner Voice Is Telling You

For a couple of days, write down everything your inner voice is telling you, because in order to change it to something productive you need to first see what your inner voice is already telling you. Write down the good, the bad, and the ugly, and you can even separate them by topic. What does your inner voice tell you about happiness? Money? Contentment? Success?

Are they words and phrases of encouragement that focus on how you can have more of those things in your life? Are they words of doubt and lack that are making you too afraid to chase those goals? Are these words that are actively putting you down, words that say you can never achieve what you desire?

There's a study that says 90% of what we do has already been programmed for us by the subconscious mind, which is the part of the mind we don't control and where the inner voice lives.

90% of what we do each day is fueled by the inner voice, and once you get the inner voice's playbook in front of you, you can focus on countering each phrase.

## Step 2: Counter Each Negative Phrase With Something Positive

It might seem a bit shocking to see all the negative phrases that your inner voice has been telling you for who knows how long, and it's had quite a while to be shaped by the environment you are in and your own thoughts. The hold it has on you and the freedom you've given it will take a while to cramp down upon, but it can be done.

First, you need to focus on the negative phrases. For example, let's take a common one that everyone seems to have when it comes to heading towards contentment: "You don't deserve to be happy." Contentment can equal happiness, or at the very least it can end the struggle that is blocking your happiness, so your mind will want to keep you from that at all costs.

A great phrase to tell yourself in order to counter that is, "I deserve happiness, and I am happy right now." Then pick out something in your life or your situation to be happy about. It doesn't matter how silly or small, you just need to pick something. It could be that the sky is blue, that you heard your favorite song on the radio, or that you are going to eat your favorite meal for dinner tonight.

It just needs to be something that will make you smile, and once that is done, you can go about your day. Every time the thought of you not deserving happiness comes up, replace the negative thought with that positive phrase and the action that causes you to feel happiness. It might take a couple of days to kick in and replace the negative thought pattern, but eventually you will find yourself not thinking that negative thought anymore.

Then you can move onto the next issue your inner voice has, turning it into an ally rather than something that will constantly tear you down. This does ask for a lot of repetition and diligence on your end, but the rewards will be well worth it.

## Having An Out Of Control Positive Inner Voice

Having an inner voice that is too positive can be a problem too, from a certain point of view. For high achievers or people who want to get things done, their inner voice can tell them to overcome challenges, climb over the next hill, and seek out the next big adventure. This isn't a bad thing at all, but it can become a problem whenever you find yourself seeking the next big adventure right on the heels of the previous one.

Satisfaction is "the fulfillment of one's wishes, expectations, or needs, or the pleasure derived from this." While you might be fulfilling your wishes and needs whenever you achieve your goals, you also need to take in the pleasure of all that you have accomplished. While you don't want to rest on your laurels for too long, you also don't want to ignore them entirely. If you've achieved a goal, then recognize and accept that goal. Feel good that you completed something so amazing, and then move onto the next one.

Tame your positive inner voice by taking a few mental steps back from the future and instead focusing on the present moment. Be present in your victory, savor the sweetness of it and the satisfaction of a job well done, and then return to the grind and finish your next goal.

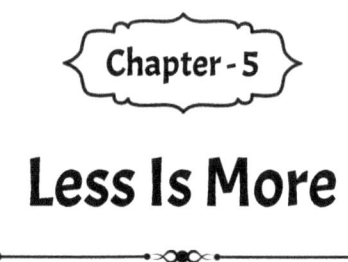

# Less Is More

One common issue some people have with satisfaction is the idea that they need more, and the need for more is something ingrained in us as young children, and it continues into adulthood. We focus on wanting and needing, and we are only satisfied when those needs are met. Yet for some, this creates a bit of a paradox. If we want more and are wired to want more, then how can we ever be satisfied if we can never have enough?

Well, some of the most satisfied people are actually those that have learned to make do with less in their lives. The idea of less is more has been around for quite a while under many different names and forms, and whether you call it decluttering, mindfulness, or minimalism, you know what it is about. Having less or having just enough to get by means that you appreciate what you have more, instead of having a lot of things you never use or take for granted.

This idea can be a lifestyle, or be a part of just one facet of your life. For example, some people strive to find satisfaction in food or in clothing, even if they only eat or buy enough to get by.

This gives them less choice in how much they eat or the number of outfits they can throw together on a given day, but it allows them to save money, improve their health, and truly value what they do have.

## How Less Is More Can Lead To Satisfaction

Think about something you like, and the amount of choice you have regarding it. For example, let's take entertainment. There're dozens of streaming services in the world, with most of them charging some sort of monthly subscription fee. Then focus on all the exclusive shows that each platform has to offer that aren't available anywhere else. Even without exclusives, what about all the classic TV shows everyone says you should watch? Plus, with all the new content that is coming out on a weekly basis?

There's just too much television to ever watch it all, and even if you had enough money to pay for every single streaming service and cable package deal out there, you wouldn't have enough time to watch everything. So, what do you do? You narrow the field by weeding out shows that don't interest you, then you figure out which streaming services are worth spending money on, and finally you look at how many hours you are devoting to each show.

Eventually, you have a much more manageable pile of television shows that are not only watchable within an understandable time frame, but are also shows that you will enjoy watching. That's an example of how less is more can lead to satisfaction, because instead of wasting time and money on shows you don't like or care for, you can spend your time on those you do… and get more fun out of it!

**This Applies To Everything**
There's a real abundance of everything right now, even if you aren't looking for it, but we are constrained by time. In order to live a contented life and have satisfaction in all of what we do, we need to focus on getting less, and we will enjoy it more without getting overwhelmed. Look at all the areas where you don't feel content, and then try to see if more or less of that is needed in your life.

Are you not satisfied at work? Perhaps you are stressed out because you are working too hard and need to dial everything back, or maybe you need to work harder and get ahead of some bigger projects to free up space and time.

Not satisfied with your family? Spend more time with them to increase your bond, or if you find yourself getting irritated by them, don't be afraid to step away and get some time for yourself.

If you haven't already guessed, one of the biggest benefits to having a more satisfying life (and one of the tools you can use) is balance in the things we do. While we as humans, hate reduction and don't want to miss out on opportunities and the next big thing, one of the things we should do is know when a little less can give us a lot more satisfaction.

You can make 'less is more' a way of life and follow it like the minimalists, or you can simply choose one area of your life and try to make some cuts. However you choose to go about it, the idea that less is more will certainly help you become more satisfied and content with your life, and might lead to other positive changes as well.

# Know When Social Media Is Toxic

# Know When Social Media Is Toxic

Social media can do a lot of good in the world, but it can also cause a lot of problems for people's mental health. From not feeling good enough, to constantly being exposed to all the hatred and petty arguments that rise to life online, to seeing only what the world wants you to see about life, social media can really make you feel unsatisfied.

While social media isn't bad on its own and can be a great tool, it is also important to know how to use social media in order to keep yourself content and not get thrown down the rabbit hole of seeing all these unrealistic expectations.

Toxic social media is real, but since the word toxic gets thrown around so much in today's world, it's best to get some definitions out of the way. First, toxic can mean poisonous, or very harmful or unpleasant in a pervasive or insidious way. If something is toxic to you, whether it is a person or an item, it is adding negativity to your life and often causing stress. So, if social media is making you sick, and you find that you close your phone and feel worse about yourself than when you started, that is toxic.

## What Is Toxic Social Media?

Toxic social media will honestly depend on the person who is using it, and what is toxic to one person might not be toxic to another. Someone might have thin skin and find mean comments on their pictures toxic, while another person who isn't affected can ignore the comments. Someone might get upset by comparing their body image to someone else online, or wonder why their life isn't as great as the latest influencer.

The causes of social media toxicity depend on a lot of things, but while what causes social media to affect people in this way differs per person, the effects are often the same across the board. People feel bad and their mental health takes a dip, they feel worthless or not as good as people on social media, or they take negative online comments to heart and quitting posting or quit a hobby they were otherwise sharing with the world.

People often report feeling terrible after being exposed to toxic social media, or often feel angry and then become toxic themselves, causing discussions to get out of hand and refusing to listen when having a debate with someone. Toxic social media will damage your quality of life, and it certainly won't help you be content!

If you find yourself feeling angry, depressed, sad, and helpless after you get off of social media, then you've probably exposed yourself to it in a toxic form. If you want to feel content with your life, then you need to fix it.

## How To Overcome Toxic Social Media

The most important thing to remember is that social media, in all its forms, is a tool run by algorithms. You are in control of what you see and experience on social media, and you can easily choose to put healthy things on your feeds and homepages.

Just like how someone wanting to overcome a toxic diet will clear out all the junk food and replace it with healthy food, you can do the same with your feeds.

Clear your internet history, unsubscribe from the channels and people and communities that you know are junk, and by doing this you reset the algorithm. Then figure out what is healthy for you on social media. Do you want to see inspiring things, messages from close family and friends only, cute animals, only things related to your business? Then start looking those things up and following communities where you can see those things. Over time, the algorithm will pick up that you are looking for health and will send you more of the same.

Then, every single time you get on social media you can walk away from your session refreshed and motivated and renewed, and not burnt out, angry, and depressed. You can turn your social media into something that helps you and doesn't hinder you, and it's something that can keep you content.

## Clearing Out The Errant Toxicity

Sometimes even the healthiest bodies get sick, and the same thing happens with social media. Sometimes something that you know is bad for you slips through the cracks, and when that happens, you can go right back to feeling bad. While you can't expect to avoid every negative thing on the internet, you can focus on what to do when that happens so it doesn't throw you off.

First, don't feed it, especially if the toxin is directed at you. Trolls, negative comments, and mean remarks are going to happen if you put yourself out there, and rather than getting angry and responding with your own anger, you can instead focus on letting go.

The best strategy is to delete the comment and walk away. Remove the toxin before it even has a chance to spread, and then don't respond to the person who posted it. Besides, that's what they want, because the people who tear others down on the internet, likely haven't built anything for themselves.

By having tools in place to prevent one bad comment or one piece of criticism from ruining your day, you can keep your mood content and you can keep using social media as a force for good regarding your mental health.

# Don't Be Afraid To Try New Things

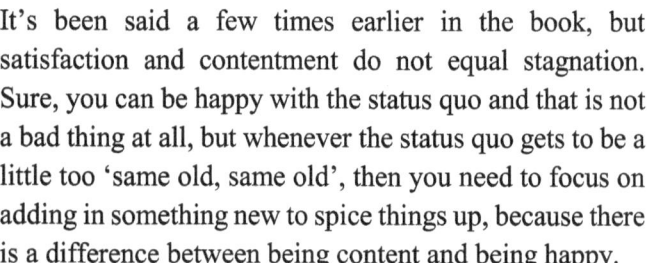

It's been said a few times earlier in the book, but satisfaction and contentment do not equal stagnation. Sure, you can be happy with the status quo and that is not a bad thing at all, but whenever the status quo gets to be a little too 'same old, same old', then you need to focus on adding in something new to spice things up, because there is a difference between being content and being happy.

Trying new things can be something that gets you out of a rut or something that introduces you to new experiences that you didn't even think you would enjoy! But what should these new things be, and how do you make sure you aren't forgetting to enjoy them?

First, take a look at your content life. What are you satisfied with? You could be satisfied that you have all your basic needs taken care of, such as enough food to eat and a roof over your head. You could also be satisfied that you have a good job and some money saved up, and that could be the excuse you need to spend a little money and try something entirely new.

But even the most content person has wishes and dreams that keep us from just existing in a content life. So think about what you want and don't be afraid to admit what you desire. You might want more adventure, more family time, or to try a new activity you are interested in. This can raise your upper limit of happiness, and trying new things can actually make you feel more content!

## The Base Level Of Happiness

The base level of happiness is a term coined by Gay Hendricks in his book "The Big Leap," where he states that we have a comfort level of happiness that is very similar to a thermostat.

When we get too hot or cold, we turn the thermostat up or down depending on what is needed to get ourselves feeling comfortable again. We do the same thing with happiness, where if we are not happy enough, we do what we can to become happy.

However, whenever we get too happy too quickly, we can self-sabotage ourselves to bring us back down to a comfort zone of happiness. An example would be getting a promotion at work, which comes with more money and more benefits. However, if we aren't prepared for this new level of happiness that the promotion provides us, then we might self-sabotage and get demoted back to our old job, just to feel comfortable and be within our means of happiness.

It sounds silly and a little crazy, but we do it all the time. However, in order to continue to live a contented life with the bad and the good that life throws at us, we need to learn to expand our base level of happiness to include when we feel really good. One of the best ways to do this is to try new things.

The base level of happiness loves a routine and a structure, and we need to shake it up by providing a brand-new thing for our lives to focus on. If you are content and happy with the way your life is so far, that doesn't mean that you don't have dreams of things you want to do, goals you want to set, or ways your life could be a little bit better. Focus on those.

## What New Things Should I Try?
Since most humans are wired to want to be better, focus on what you want to be better at. For example, let's say you are content with your body. You like the way it looks and you aren't comparing yourself to anyone else. However, you also decide that you could be a bit fitter and at least strong enough to PR your next barbell lift at the gym, so maybe try a new gym routine, diet, and workout plan to get stronger.

Or maybe you are content with your relationship but want to open up more and focus on sharing one another's interests. Maybe try a new activity together, or plan alternating dates where you each pick an activity you want to share with the other.

Trying new things doesn't have to be a grand declaration of a lifestyle altering goal, or something that will push you past satisfaction and into more stress to be the best, but it should be something you should feel excited and passionate about. It should also be something that you can feel happy about when you complete it.

Remember, you are trying to raise your base level of happiness and contentment around this new activity, and not get too stressed out over it.

# Life Is A Journey, Not A Destination

# Life Is A Journey, Not A Destination

Have you ever been on a really peaceful car ride? Not the one where the road trip is one from hell and you would give anything to get to your destination and make it end, but the kind of road trip that just puts you in a trance? The kind that makes you smile and drive around, stopping at all the cool places on the side of the road, listening to content that you enjoy, and focusing on the drive itself?

Sometimes it can be very hard to give up a trip and actually get to the destination. Well, life is like that too. It can seem like everyone is always chasing something, whether it's more money, time, fame, fortune, glory, or respect, and that chase can end up driving them crazy. They are so fixated on the end result that they forget to stop and smell the roses on the side of the road.

Life isn't a destination, although it sometimes seem that way, but life's only endpoint is death, and this author can imagine that everyone wants to stay as far away from that destination as possible. Feeling contentment and happiness is one of the best ways to ensure that you squeeze as much out of the journey as possible, and having a life where you can say "I'm satisfied" is the first step.

## Focus On What Really Matters

As much as we might want to keep up with the Joneses and buy stuff, we don't need to impress people we don't like. One of the best ways to make memories on this journey is to connect with everyone making the journey with us. While chasing money and power and fame is fine and can help you make connections, you don't want to forgo the human element entirely.

Meet new people in your life and connect with old ones, fall in love, make friends, find mentors, and talk about everything under the sun. One of the best ways to feel almost instant satisfaction is to look someone in the eyes after you have helped them out. It's an amazing feeling, because whether you helped them move or helped them solve a tormenting problem, you got to play a role in their story.

Making other people's lives better is one of the best things you can do on the journey, and it will aid your own mental health too. While it seems like the world can be more divided than ever, a few good deeds and actions will be more than enough to bring your little corner of the world together.

## Don't Be Afraid To Rest And Just Be Content

Do you remember the feeling during your first rest stop after a few hours in the car? Sometimes there's nothing more glorious than stretching your legs, using the bathroom, walking around a new environment, and fueling up with both gas and food for the road ahead. It's almost a spiritual experience to just rest for a bit before you get back on the road, and the same concept applies towards the road trip of life as well.

Sometimes we are so focused on the idea of being satisfied or the idea of contentment that we don't actually stop and allow ourselves to feel those emotions. We are chasing ideas without knowing that they aren't ideas. They are feelings that are deep inside of us, and we can feel them free of charge.

So, while you are going through life, make a note of when you feel satisfied and content, and then take the time to feel those feelings. If you find yourself ignoring the feelings in favor of chasing the ideas, then just like with a rest stop, schedule your rest. Taking a few minutes every day to look at all you have, feel gratitude, and be content with enough can refresh your mind, body, and soul.

After that, you can get back on life's road and keep on traveling to your next destination.

## Have Some Fun

Finally, being content and satisfied, without being connected to any emotions caused by your expectations can be very fun. You don't want more, you don't have less, and that's a cause for celebration! However, just like with rest, we often don't allow ourselves to be happy that we have enough, and we save the parties for whenever we have an excess of money or fame or time.

But being content means that you don't have chains binding you to feelings of lack, scarcity, and you aren't constantly comparing yourself to others and beating yourself up. That's a cause for celebration, so don't be afraid to make a party out of what you have. Do something fun, practice self-love, and really appreciate all of the things you worked hard to get.

# Conclusion

# Conclusion

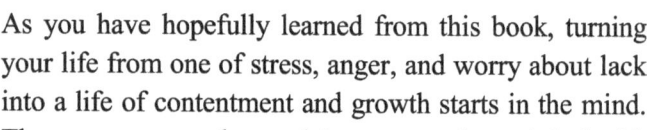

As you have hopefully learned from this book, turning your life from one of stress, anger, and worry about lack into a life of contentment and growth starts in the mind. The sooner you understand that you can be satisfied with anything and with any part of a situation, even the negative parts, the sooner you can focus on becoming a satisfied human being.

It's going to take some time and require changing habits that might have taken years to become automatic, but once you make those changes, silence your inner voice, purge toxicity from your life, and accept that life is one big journey, you will have a more contented life and lifestyle.

Plus, the mindset of satisfaction will never be able shake from you once you get it locked in your brain as the default mode. So, no matter what life throws at you next, you will be able to enjoy it and keep your emotions satisfied.

www.ingramcontent.com/pod-product-compliance
Lightning Source LLC
LaVergne TN
LVHW061603070526
838199LV00077B/7157